Symbols of Faith

Symbols of Faith

A LENTEN DEVOTIONAL FOR AFRICAN AMERICAN CHURCHES AND FAMILIES

written by
AFRICAN AMERICAN SCHOLARS, PASTORS, AND LAY LEADERS

compiled by
CHARISSE L. GILLETT

edited by
TANYA J. TYLER

Print: 9780827235700

EPUB: 9780827235717

EPDF: 9780827235724

ChalicePress.com

Printed in the United States of America

CONTENTS

Introduction

Hello, friends.

Symbols of Faith: A Lenten Journey, like *Melodies of Faith: An Advent Devotional for African American Churches and Families,* is written by scholars, church leaders, educators, and laity rooted in the African American experience. Advent and Lent are the seasons that draw us to remember the birth, life, death, and resurrection of Jesus Christ.

Lent represents the forty-day period that starts with Ash Wednesday and leads to Easter. It is a time of reflection on Jesus' ministry through the themes of prayer, repentance, fasting, and almsgiving. As we remember and reflect, we confront the reality of our lives as African Americans; Africans in America; and, most importantly, children of God. The contributing authors share their understandings of who God is, why Jesus matters, and how, in the face of enormous odds, African Americans continue to embrace a God who simply is. *Symbols of Faith* prepares us for Good Friday and Easter Sunday through imagery drawn from movies, music, flowers, African symbols, personal narratives, ashes, and more. During Lent, we experience Jesus' journey to the cross. *Symbols of Faith* is an invitation to go deeper. Thank you for accepting our invitation.

With hope,

Dr. Charisse L. Gillett

Starting Anew from the Ashes

The Lord has anointed me ... to give them a garland instead of ashes. —Isaiah 61:1, 3

The wood-burning stove at Great-Grandmother Lizzie's house always seemed to be burning, even in summer. It brought me comfort whenever we went to visit her. The ashes had to be cleaned out to start a new fire. Ashes in scripture symbolize grief, seeking forgiveness, humility, lament—and harm and humiliation. We see ashes used to reveal harm and humiliation in the story of Tamar in 2 Samuel 13:1–19. Tamar was King David's daughter and Absalom's sister. Tamar and Absalom had a brother by another mother, Amnon. Amnon raped Tamar. Scripture reveals Tamar "put ashes on her head, and tore the long robe that she was wearing; she put her hand on her head and went away, crying aloud as she went. Her brother Absalom heard her" (2 Samuel 13:19). He came and took her home with him. God loves us not because we are perfect, but because God is love.

Reflection: Who in your community needs attention? How might you help them lift their eyes to see God in their midst?

Prayer: Holy creating God, may the residue from our ashes this year start a new fire in us. Enable us to see the ashes of others and be your helpers in works of love, healing, and justice, like Jesus. Amen.

Rev. Joan Bell Haynes is former interim regional minister of the Christian Church (Disciples of Christ) in Georgia.

Dust in God's Hands

It was you who formed my inward parts.
—Psalms 139:13 (English Standard Version)

Ash Wednesday is day of remembrance: "You are dust, and to dust you shall return" (Genesis 3:19). These words press us to pause and recognize our frailty. Psalm 139 reminds us we are not just any dust—we are dust *formed* by the hands of God. Fashioned in love. Woven with intention. Infused with purpose.

As Black people living the Black experience, we know what it means to carry dust on our skin and dignity in our soul. We've been pressed low by the weight of oppression, yet the Spirit of God lifts us up. We've walked through dry places—wildernesses of racism, economic struggle, and spiritual warfare. And still we have seen the goodness of the Lord in the land of the living.

Psalm 139 speaks of a God who knows us—every thought, every step, every moment before it ever comes to pass. God knows our weariness, our wanderings, our wilderness. Yet the same God who sees our dust loves us with everlasting love. Not because we are perfect, but because we are known—and still chosen.

Lent is a season of stripping away, of quiet surrender. But it is also a season of remembering: we are not forgotten. Our dust ain't just any old kind of dust. Dust in God's hands becomes a miracle.

Despite all the evil in this world and the evil in our hearts, we are walking miracles. We are made in the image and likeness of God. With intention. With love. With purpose. With the assurance that even in our most broken places, God is near.

Reflection: How can your village help you walk this Lenten season with humility, courage, and trust?

Prayer: O Lord, you formed us from the dust and breathed life into us. In this Lenten season, help us return to you with an open heart. Remind us that even in our lowliness, we are known and loved. Amen.

Rev. Cherisna Jean-Marie is dean of Disciples Divinity House at Vanderbilt in Nashville, Tennessee.

Seeing the Red-Eemable

Though your sins are like scarlet, they shall be like snow; though they are red like crimson, they shall become like wool. —Isaiah 1:18

Confession is a spiritual concept connected with the Lenten season. I must confess I've been seeing red since the November 2024 presidential election. When America chose a candidate set on whitewashing and rolling back history, I started seeing red. The deportation of a Hispanic mother and daughter who frequented our church's weekly Meal Connect ministry because of the administration's immigration antics has me seeing red. Knowing the hardship many must endure as a result of the "Big Ugly Bill" has me seeing red. Yes, I confess, I am angry! Isaiah 1:18 tells me I'm in good company.

The wickedness, injustice, and corruption in Judah and Jerusalem and the nation's political pollution and economic oppression had God seeing red in Isaiah 1. God was angry because the hands of money-hungry politicians and bought-off judges were covered with innocent blood. However, God didn't just see red when looking at the abhorrent sociopolitical and socioeconomic crises engulfing Judah's communities. God also saw the *RED*-eemable. God dispatched the prophet Isaiah to the nation's capital, Jerusalem, with an incredible message: Though their sins were red as crimson, they were redeemable. God made individual and social redemption possible through the cross-work of the Suffering Servant of Isaiah 53. Although I'm seeing RED, thanks be to God I also see the *RED*-eemable.

Reflection: The cross-work of Jesus motivated Rev. Dr. Martin Luther King Jr.; he believed unearned suffering was redemptive. What does your belief in the cross-work of Christ motivate you to do?

Prayer: Thank you, Father, for loving the world so much that you sent your Son to us. Even when we see red, help us to also see the red-eemable. Amen.

Rev. Dr. Nathl L. Moore is pastor of First African Baptist Church in Lexington, Kentucky.

Reflection on the Color Black

As long as I am in the world, I am the light of the world.
—John 9:5

Imagine giving up color for Lent. Would that mean only wearing black? Black is scientifically understood as the absence of color because black absorbs light and doesn't reflect the various colors of the light spectrum. Yet we still think of black as a color because our eyes can perceive it.

Black as a color can be a powerful image for the Lenten season. During this forty-day period, we engage in spiritual reflection. Often, by giving up something, we reflect on the experience of lack and what it means to rely more heavily on our faith to sustain us. This isn't an outward reflection. It is inner reflection of deep contemplation. Much like Jesus' journey in the wilderness, going without is a spiritual practice. We learn to focus on what is most important in our lives and what sustains us.

Black as the lack of color pushes us to reflect more deeply on our understanding of Jesus Christ as the Light of the world. He is not merely light all around us, but light inside of us, too. Jesus is the light we absorb and the light we experience as inner peace and calm. We carry this light within us even during the darkest of times. It is also a light that is in us when we are tempted and when we are in doubt.

Black is a point of reflection. Just as it absorbs and contains all light, through faith we absorb the light of Christ. We have a light within that sustains and inspires us always.

Reflection: What unwarranted contrasts are you making on your faith journey? In your life? Why?

Prayer: Dear God, may we continue to reflect on how our faith sustains us through the Lenten season, even as we await the full light of Easter. Give us the vision to reflect and journey to the light. Amen.

Rev. B. Chris Dorsey is president of Disciples Home Missions.

Noticing Purple

When you fast, put oil on your head and wash your face.
—Matthew 6:17

Purple is more than just a color; it's a statement. It represents power, royalty, and sovereignty. It evokes dignity and reverence with deep spiritual meaning. During Lent, purple also reminds us of Jesus' solidarity with those on the social margins.

Alice Walker in *The Color Purple* wrote, "I think it pisses God off if you walk by the color purple in a field somewhere and don't notice it." We need to recognize divine beauty everywhere, especially in places often overlooked. We need to see the "purple" in our spiritual lives—the hidden, internal, and truly valuable.

For those of us who navigate a world that scrutinizes our worth on the basis of racism, heterosexism, or misogyny, Jesus' message resonates deeply. Our spiritual practices, built on resilience, are not for external validation. When we seek to impress, we weaken the deep, silent strength and integrity of our spiritual journey. True spiritual "purple," genuine royalty in God's kin-dom, lies not in public displays but in the powerful authenticity of our hearts, shown through unwavering resistance, self-preservation, and radical love.

For generations, Black and Brown people, especially women, have bravely challenged systems designed to limit access and silence their voices. Jesus calls us to build a lasting legacy. Are we investing in the eternal "purple" of God's kin-dom—a lasting glory rooted in our steadfast integrity, vibrant communities, and fierce pursuit of liberation for all? Let us embrace purple as a symbol of the inherent royalty that awakens when our hearts align with God's justice.

Reflection: How might the pressure to perform or be seen in dominant societal structures impact your authentic spiritual practices?

Prayer: Ever-living, ever-loving God, strengthen us during this Lenten season to embrace resilience in the face of struggles for justice and liberation. In Jesus' name we pray. Amen.

Rev. Dr. Leslie Carole Taylor is senior minister at First Christian Church (Disciples of Christ) in Concord, California.

Royal Blood, Redeeming Love

They clothed him in a purple cloak. —Mark 15:17

In the Black church, Lent has a sound, a feel, a look. You hear it in the hymns and spirituals that slow our pace and steady our hearts. You feel it in the solemnity of worship, the quiet urgency of prayer, the intentional acts of giving. And you see it in the colors.

Purple and red preach their own sermon. Purple, once rare and costly, was the color of kings and queens. In scripture, the soldiers draped a purple robe on Jesus in mockery. They didn't know they were cloaking the King of kings. In African American history, our ancestors wore purple on Easter Sunday as an act of defiance and dignity, declaring, "We are royalty in God's kingdom," even when the world denied their worth.

Red tells another story—of sacrifice. It is the color of Christ's blood, shed for the sins of the world. It is the color of the communion cloth that rests on the table in many of our sanctuaries. It calls to mind the lamb's blood on the doorposts in Exodus. And in our history, red also whispers of the blood of those who labored, fought, and died.

Together, purple and red remind us that Lent is both crown and cross, dignity and deliverance. They remind us that our Savior is both sovereign and suffering—glorious enough to command the heavens, humble enough to wash feet.

Every time we cover the table in red or dress the sanctuary in purple, we tell the story again: We are loved enough to be redeemed and valued enough to be crowned.

Reflection: Where do you see God's dignity (purple) and redemption (red) at work in your life?

Prayer: Lord Jesus, King in purple, Lamb in red, thank you for crowning us with mercy and covering us with grace. Help us walk humbly, love deeply, and live boldly, remembering the price you paid. Amen.

Rev. Tara Faith Williams is pastor of New Covenant Church (Disciples of Christ) in Nashville, Tennessee.

A Sacrifice of Love

As he watched Jesus walk by, he exclaimed, "Look, here is the Lamb of God!" —John 1:36

Imagine the hush that fell over the crowd when John the Baptist pointed and declared, "Look! The Lamb of God!" It wasn't just a poetic phrase—it was a bold proclamation. With those words, John identified Jesus not just as a teacher or prophet but as the fulfillment of centuries of hope, sacrifice, and prophecy.

In the Old Testament, spotless lambs were brought to the altar as sacrifices, their blood a temporary covering for sin. But Jesus —the perfect, sinless Lamb—came to do what no animal sacrifice ever could: remove sin entirely. Once. For all. Forever.

This wasn't a distant, ritualistic act. It was deeply personal. Jesus knew what it would cost him, and he chose the cross anyway. That kind of love can't be measured—it can only be received with awe and gratitude.

When we call Jesus the Lamb of God, we're reminded of both his purity and his sacrifice. He was innocent, yet he bore our guilt. He was sinless, yet he became sin for us. His blood didn't just cover our mistakes—it cleansed us completely.

Today, pause and remember: your freedom was bought with his life. Let that truth move you—not just to tears, but to transformation.

Reflection: How does knowing Jesus gave his life as the Lamb of God change the way you live today?

Prayer: Jesus, thank you for being the Lamb who took my place. Let the weight of your sacrifice never grow light in my heart. Teach me to live in the freedom and joy of your love, surrendered and grateful. Amen.

Rev. Dr. Freddie Lawton Sr. is regional minister of the Christian Church (Disciples of Christ) in South Carolina.

Beautiful Contradictions

Like a lamb that is led to the slaughter, and like a sheep that before its shearers is silent, so he did not open his mouth.
—Isaiah 53:7

When I was a girl, my mom would buy us a beautiful bunny cake coated in coconut for Easter. Our hair freshly pressed, we wore frilly dresses, ruffled socks, and little white gloves on Easter morning.

Easter was a time of sweetness—baskets filled with jellybeans and eggs, Easter speeches recited by little children. The lambs, ducklings, and bunnies in storybooks and decorations seemed to reflect the gentle innocence of Jesus, the Lamb of God.

But my parents made sure we also understood the more profound meaning of Easter. Jesus, the true Lamb, laid down his life for the sins of the world. When I think of him, so many beautiful contradictions come to mind.

The Lamb is innocent and docile, yet Jesus was also the Lion, strong enough to carry a cross and endure betrayal and death. The same Jesus who was led like a lamb to the slaughter is also our Ram in the bush: fierce, powerful, and willing to fight for our redemption.

Though my childhood memory recalls the sweet aspects of Eastertide, I am reminded that growing up has ushered me away from innocence and into life's complexities. Lent, through the Lamb of God, calls us back to the purity we once knew. It invites us to let go of pride, bitterness, and fear and embrace the childlike heart that first believed.

Reflection: What contradictions live in you?

Prayer: Lord, help me surrender what stands in the way of becoming more like You. Thank You for being the Lamb who was led to slaughter, so I might live. Amen.

Minister Cynthia Newman is acting director of strategic engagement and assistant vice president for Disciples Overseas Ministries.

From Adoration to Action

"Here is the Lamb of God who takes away the sin of the world!" —John 1:29

Recently I went to my neighborhood health club to renew my membership. To do so, I needed technical support. The staff member requested my mobile phone and in less than a minute renewed my membership. As I was walking toward the workout area, the staff member stopped me, asking, "Are you a believer?" I asked them why the question? They said, "I saw the Bible app on your phone and thought you might be a believer." I said yes, although that term believer is not cultural for me. I was drawn to the question: "Why do we often use superficial explanations to speak about symbols representing God and Jesus? Does having a Bible make me or you a 'believer'?"

As I reflected on this question, the symbol of the Lamb came to mind. In John 1:29, John the Baptist describes Jesus as the One who will atone for the sins of humanity. Perhaps we can go deeper in this Lenten season and see the Lamb active in the world today. Perhaps we can use our spiritual imagination to envision the Lamb of God as present with us as we engage in transformative thinking. Perhaps we can learn to see the Lamb of God as a living force who requires our active participation. The Lamb of God becomes the disruptor of the empire who walks with us as we advocate against racism, sexism, sexual and domestic violence, and systemic oppression. The Lamb of God liberates the church to engage in theological discernment that moves toward hearing the call to live the abundant life. He is the sufferer, yes, but he is also the One who suffers with us. Now we can move closer to the the Lamb who exposes the sin of the world. Our call is to embody this mission across generations, for as John 14:12 says: You "will do greater works than these."

Reflection: Where must we show up, not as passive believers but as radical disciples?

Prayer: Lord, grant us the courage and strength to move toward the work of the radical "Lamb of God"—our mission from generation to generation.

Sharon Ellis Davis, M.Div., DMin., PhD, is an assistant visiting professor of pastoral ethics at Lexington Theological Seminary.

Hope Amid Suffering

I lift up my eyes to the hills—from where will my help come?
—Psalms 121:1

Psalms 121:1–8 appears to paint a picture of hope in an all-powerful God who watches our lives 24/7, promising no harm will come to our bodies. The reality is that harm in the form of unexplained suffering has happened to bodies throughout time, all over the world, seemingly with no reprieve. Where is hope in those moments?

As an African American woman, I wonder how "hope in the moment" happened amid chattel slavery, Jim Crow, Jane Crow, and segregation. Where is hope as we witness suffering through the mass deportation of mostly Black and Brown bodies, atrocities in Gaza and elsewhere, natural disasters, cancer wards, mass shootings, and loss?

In *The Magician's Nephew,* C.S. Lewis tells of a boy named Digory who asks Aslan the Lion to heal his dying mother. Digory pleads repeatedly, receiving no response. Looking down at the lion's feet, he sees an all-powerful being who knew no defeat. But when Digory looks up at the lion's face, he sees great shining tears. Aslan felt his pain and showed divine empathy—love and hope amid suffering, with relief appearing in unexpected places.

Lewis helped me realize that when I see God only as all-powerful, shielding, and rescuing, I miss the intimacy of the One who cries with me and is present 24/7, waiting until suffering ends, providing relief like the kindness and gentleness of a dove. The Lord is close to the broken-hearted and feels our pain (Psalms 34:18). We worship a God who is all-powerful to protect and a God who cries even unto the cross.

Reflection: When have you recalled the Lord's presence amid suffering? What symbol of hope was present in that moment?

Prayer: Lord, help us this Lenten season to open ourselves to be with those hurting around us. Show us how our tears and presence can serve as a dove, symbolizing your presence filled with empathy, hope, and peace. Amen.

Rev. Dr. A. Denise Bell is Donald and Lillian Nunnelly endowed chair of pastoral leadership at Lexington Theological Seminary.

In Search of the Dove: Facing Fear

He who keeps you will not slumber. —Psalms 121:3

Psalm 121 reflects Israel's life in exile. The psalmist is trapped in a distant land with an uncertain future, but he trusts God has something better in store.

Fear grips and arrests our thoughts, impedes progress, and stifles imagination. Fear entices us, causes worry and uncertainty, and blurs our vision. Fear was central to my vocational discernment. I was in Haiti, a relative youngster in a group of experienced global church leaders who were regularly confronted with the inequalities of poverty and despair. Yet they maintained faith in God's abiding love and presence in ways I hadn't seen or experienced.

Fear visited me and confronted me with insecurities about my powerlessness. I surrendered. I lay on the floor helpless, wrestling with both fear and God. Like the psalmist, I had a choice: let this situation consume me or look for God's presence. Then the Spirit visited me, reminding me that sharing in and with this community was transformative. I was reminded that our help is in God's abiding love and presence. A dove descended that night, bringing peace to my soul and purpose to my life.

The dove is a symbol of peace and transformation after seasons of turmoil or uncertainty. It marks a transition into hope. The dove was Noah's symbol that the flood was over and God's new work was imminent. The dove appeared at Jesus' baptism, demonstrating redemption for humanity. Jesus' vocational journey models for us the act of relinquishing fear to the anticipation of God's work and will in this world. In seasons of fear and trauma, we must look for symbols of hope.

Reflection: What fears are you facing for yourself, your family, and/or your community? Where might you find a dove in the midst of transformation and fear?

Prayer: Holy God, as we find ourselves in seasons of fear and disorientation, open our eyes to see symbols of your abiding love and presence. Amen.

Rev. Monica Wedlock Kilpatrick is vice president of organizational and leadership development at National Benevolent Association.

In the Secret Place with God

Whenever you pray, go into your room and shut the door and pray to your Father who is in secret. —Matthew 6:6

In the Sermon on the Mount, Jesus calls us back to the roots of the spiritual disciplines, teaching us to make time to put them into practice. Jesus warns against self-righteousness and pride. We must not be presumptuous do-gooders, praying to be applauded and fasting to be seen. Instead, Jesus invites us to enter the quiet, hidden places where only God can see the frailty of our human hearts.

During Lent, we are invited to enter a deeper, more honest intimacy with God. Whether we are giving, praying, or fasting, the purpose is not to call attention to our own actions but to solidify and deepen our relationships with God and one another. For me, this happens in what is called "the secret place"—also known as the backside of the desert. There you will find no crowds cheering, no lights blinking, no cameras rolling. The only applause heard is the angels rejoicing over someone's decision to follow Jesus. There you will find only one type of communion: the inner communing with God.

Jesus says, "Where our treasure is, there our hearts will be also" (Matthew 6:21). Lent asks us to look at what we have decided to treasure. It invites us to pay attention to those things that create divided loyalties. Are we storing up approval, status, comfort - or are we storing up trust in God's love and presence? We are called not to impress the world but to draw nearer to the One whose Kin-dom has no end, the One who is with us in transformative ways—quiet, profound, and eternal.

Reflection: In this Lenten season, have you given thought to how you will find time to hear God's voice? Where is your quiet place?

Prayer: Holy God, draw us into the quiet places where we can hear your voice and feel your presence. In secret, may our souls find shape in your Spirit. In public, may we manifest the depths of Your Kin-dom. Amen.

Rev. Dr. Christal L. Williams is regional minister of the Christian Church (Disciples of Christ) in Indiana.

A Reflection on Desert Journeys

All along my pilgrim journey, Lord, I want Jesus to walk with me. —Traditional African American spiritual

Jesus was in the desert, the wilderness, for forty days, communing with God and preparing for his public ministry.

I have intentionally walked or driven into several deserts in my lifetime. All with a clear goal, purpose, or destination in mind.

Driving from Oklahoma to Southern California through the Chihuahuan, Sonoran, and Mojave deserts to a new home. Miles and miles of lush, green landscapes gave way to hot, dry terrain. And just when we thought the desert trek was done, we learned that California, the place we now call home, is a desert!

Walking the eastern desert of Egypt near St. Anthony's Monastery to take the 120 steps up to St. Anthony's Cave, to sit where he secluded himself for days to pray. Sideways was the only way to squeeze through the narrow entrance. Once inside, a flashlight was needed to see the place where the hermit saint would sit, recline, or kneel to pray.

An evening hike in the Judean desert to watch the sunset. At the top of the mountain, some focused on the Dead Sea to the east while others gave their full attention to the sun slowly leaving the sky.

A constant prayer accompanied each desert journey:

All along this pilgrim journey,
Lord, I want Jesus to walk with me.

Reflection: What desert journeys have you taken in your life? Who was your companion who helped get you through the desert to the other side?

Prayer: Hear this lament of deep longing for Jesus' presence during Lent as a prayer:

Walk with me, Jesus, as I seek place, a new home.

Walk with me, Jesus, as I squeeze through the tight spaces in life.

Walk with me, Jesus, when I need a nudge to remind me to face in the direction that keeps you in sight. Amen.

Rev. Dr. Belva Brown Jordan is former moderator of the Christian Church (Disciples of Christ).

Into the Wilderness

Then Jesus was led up by the Spirit into the wilderness to be tempted by the devil. —Matthew 4:1

Not far from the church I serve in Ruidoso, New Mexico, is White Sands National Monument. According to its website, the park is composed of gypsum sand engulfing 275 square miles of desert, creating the world's largest gypsum dune field. The dunes rise high above the road, stark and bright under the relentless sun. The park appears barren and lifeless, but you can see the brave yucca plants struggling to establish roots and grow. Various types of cacti, reptiles, and rodents also thrive in this harsh environment. If you're lucky, you may see a blue lizard darting along the sand. What will grab your senses most is the *silence.* The wind blows, erasing your footsteps from the landscape, but you can barely hear it. It opens a space for you to listen to the musings of your heart.

I wonder if this is the type of wilderness where the Spirit took Jesus immediately after his baptism. The desert is an ideal place to prepare your heart and soul for the challenges that lie ahead. The Spirit knew that in the quiet and barrenness Jesus could pray and listen for God's voice to reassure and instruct him. At night, the stars would cover the sky above him with fierce majesty, an awesome display of God's power and creativity. There was no better place for Jesus to get ready for the wonderful adventure God had planned for him.

Reflection: Where will you go to prepare your heart for your next God-given adventure?

Prayer: God, you did not abandon Jesus in the desert. You were there with him to prepare him for his beautiful destiny. Be with us in our desert wanderings and wonderings. Prepare our hearts to follow and serve you. Amen.

Rev. Tanya J. Tyler is pastor of First Christian Church (Disciples of Christ) in Ruidoso, New Mexico.

Eyes Lifted in the Desert

He who keeps you will not slumber. —*Psalms 121:3*

Lent can pull us into a desert kind of experience—a place of dryness, silence, reflection, and deep soul-searching. During Lent, we remember Jesus' forty days of fasting and testing in the wilderness. Although the desert may seem barren, empty, and stagnant, it is powerfully rich with the transformative presence of God.

Psalm 121 reminds us that even in the most desolate or loneliest of places, our help comes from God. The One who made heaven and earth is not far from us. God is the keeper of our hearts, souls, and minds. God does not sleep nor slumber.

Red, which is often seen during Lent, symbolizes pressure, pain, and a promise. It is the hue of suffering—of bloodshed, of sacrifices made. But red is also the color or mark of deep love, of the fire of the Holy Spirit, and of poured-out life that cannot be quenched.

As we journey from the ashes of Lent toward the hallowed tomb of Easter, we are reminded that resurrection does not bypass the desert—it rises from within it in victory, marveling in its blessing. The deserts of our lives will lead our souls to a holy quenching. God watches over us in that desert. That same God rolls away stones and breathes new life into dead spirits. Look up!

***Reflection*: What is preventing you from looking up?**

Prayer: Great God of the desert, when the way is hard and the days are long, help us lift our eyes to you. Bring us through the wilderness of Lent, preparing our hearts for the joy of resurrection. Amen.

Rev. Dr. Christal L. Williams is regional minister for the Christian Church (Disciples of Christ) in Indiana.

The Real Weight-Loss Plan

Present your bodies as a living sacrifice, holy and acceptable to God. —Romans 12:1

My early Lenten experiences centered on one frequently asked question: What are you giving up for Lent? Most often, the responses I heard focused on fasting from certain foods for the purpose of weight loss. For many, Lent was the gateway to a summer makeover!

Ultimately, I came to understand that Lent calls us to a clearer, more consistent, and more credible connection with Christ Jesus, even as we contend with the hardcore realities of our world and our ways of functioning within our world.

During Lent, we acknowledge the uneasy peace accord we sign daily between our faith and our world. Our faith seeks an all-access pass to our very being. It is a faith with nonnegotiable requirements of mutuality, love, justice, and peace.

Conversely, our world hungers for destructive, imposter realities of selfishness, schism, and supremacy. The world accepts as collateral damage the poverty, discrimination, under-funded schools, and inadequate health care that upends our communities, particularly through big-and-not-so-beautiful legislation.

The apostle Paul recognized our plight as he addressed the Roman Christians in Romans 12:1–2. Considering Paul's words, I realize Lent's true weight-loss plan calls for eliminating the comfort-driven, status-quo-accepting agreements we have made with life the way it is. Now we can live as Christ's agents of mutuality, love, justice, and peace. Lent is a call for transformation.

Reflection: What are you giving up for Lent? How will your sacrifice position you to live as one of Christ's agents for mutuality, love, justice, and peace?

Prayer: God of life, love, and liberation, draw us closer to you so that we may live as Christ's ambassadors for justice and influencers for equity. Amen.

Rev. Dr. Jack Sullivan Jr., DMin, DHL,
is an adjunct instructor at the Center for Ministry and Lay Training, Phillips Theological Seminary, and lives in Columbus, Ohio.

Fasting by Faith, Not for Fame

Whenever you fast, do not look somber, like the hypocrites.
—Matthew 6:1

Matthew 6 offers a radical re-centering of spiritual practice. Jesus, speaking to a people under the weight of imperial occupation and religious performance, calls his followers to a righteousness not performed before others but perfected in God's presence. Fasting, then, is not spiritual theater; it is sacred surrender.

In the Black Louisiana tradition, especially in places like Opelousas, fasting has never been a hallowed ritual. It is a way of bearing witness to faith amid suffering. It is communal and contemplative, shaped by shared memory and cultural expression. Our ancestors fasted not only for spiritual refinement but for survival and liberation. Their fasts were not performative; they were prophetic. Fasting was a way to align the body and soul with God's justice. It was a cry for divine intervention when the courts failed, when the schools were segregated, when hunger persisted and healing seemed out of reach. It was both lament and liberation.

Jesus' words here challenge both ancient and modern performances of piety. He urges us to return to the secret place within. We fast not to be seen, but to see more clearly. We fast not to impress, but to embody the humility of Christ. The God who sees in secret is the God who gives peace in the storm, clarity in the chaos, and power in the wilderness.

***Reflection*:** How might fasting reconnect you with the wisdom and resilience of our spiritual ancestors?

Prayer: God, you met our ancestors in fields of oppression. You meet me now in this quiet room of devotion. Teach me to fast as Jesus taught—not to be noticed by others, but to be near you. Amen.

Rev. Dr. Michael L. Zachary Sr. is author of From Soil to Soul: The Impact of Community Gardens on Food Insecurity and lives in Lexington, Kentucky.

No One Else But God

Know that the Lord is God. —Psalms 100:3

On an African immersion experience, while driving through Accra, Ghana, we kept seeing a symbol. It was shaped like an anchor, but the hook was on both ends. It was visible, unique, and beautiful, by far the most popular symbol in the Ghanian culture.

Riding on an old, raggedy bus with the windows down, feeling the wind blow through the aisles, I asked Professor Boykins Sanders, our host, what the symbol meant. He stood up excitedly and said, "It is an African Adinka symbol that means '*Gye Nyame*.'" I asked, "What does that mean?" He said, "The Supremacy of God. No one else except God. Except for God, I would not be."

The Ghanaians believe that when you look at all the issues in life, beginning with our ancestors and slavery, the devastation, the heartaches, the poverty, trying to make it day by day, nothing matters, no one else matters, except God.

On American soil, our ancestors knew something about symbols. They told us about a God who sits high and looks low. They told us about a God who opens doors no one can close and closes doors no one can open. They told us Jesus is our shelter in the storm. They told us "trouble don't last always."

They told us about a symbol that reveals God's Spirit in us. "On a hill far away stood an old rugged cross, the emblem of suffering and shame. ... I love that old cross, where the dearest and best for a world of lost sinners was slain."[1]

Reflection: What symbols have invited you to see the suffering and pain of the cross with new eyes?

Prayer: Dear God, we thank you for the symbols that remind us that we belong to you. Besides you, there is no other God. Amen.

Rev. Dr. Nadine Burton is vice president of development for the Great Lakes zone of the Christian Church Foundation.

[1] George Bennard, "The Old Rugged Cross," 1912.

On the Way

The Lord is your shade at your right hand. —Psalms 121:5

Rev. Terri Hord Owens writes in her Lenten devotional, *Facing Jerusalem,* "Jesus is on His way to His ultimate purposes, facing His 'Jerusalem moments' all along the way."2 How do we move forward when a mountainous decision is ahead of us? Where do we take refuge or find solace when what we are facing is seemingly insurmountable? The psalmist suggests we sing, allowing our souls to sustain us by making melody in our hearts to the Lord. He reminds us the source of our help and strength is not outside of us but within us. We can sing and shout and reimagine the mountains as a sanctuary.

The Lenten season stirs churches around the nation to fast and pray, sacrifice some hidden or private struggle, or "lay aside every weight and the sin that clings so closely" (Hebrews 12:1)—only for forty days, mind you. This practice of sacrifice is our offering. It veils the agony and shame of the Via Dolorosa and the ultimate joy and beauty of Resurrection Sunday.

David, our ancient psalmist, used his musical pen to incite us to rejoice in who God is—our protector, our sentinel, our shade, our keeper. We must sing while we are on the way toward what is ahead, despite what is ahead, and, as our modern-day psalmist Richard Smallwood writes, in total praise for what is ahead.

Reflection: What mountains have you faced recently? Did you face them with courage and faith?

Prayer: Father, you created us to join with all nature in manifold witness to your great splendor, majesty, and might. We now look forward to ushering in your kingdom on earth, as it is in heaven. Amen.

Rev. Walter Owens Jr. is minster of the creative arts ministry at Salem Baptist Church of Chicago, Illinois.

[2] Terri Hord Owens, *Facing Jerusalem: A Lenten Journey with Jesus* (St. Louis: Chalice Press, 2025).

Still Our Refuge

By the rivers of Babylon ... there we wept when we remembered Zion. —Psalms 137:1

Almost all of my local family attended Galilee Christian Church. This is the church where both my parents accepted their calls to ministry. My older brothers and I were all baptized there on the same day. This is the church where my grandfather, Elder Adam Holman, knelt in prayer, often ending by asking God "to save a seat in God's kingdom" for him and his desire "to hear God say 'Well done, thou good and faithful servant.'"

Granddaddy taught me by example to serve God's people. He found work and provided transportation for relatives and friends. They'd pick cucumbers, beans, watermelons, peanuts, peaches, and more in fields owned by White people in this Lowcountry South Carolina community. These exhausted people—who traveled up to sixty miles for work—still found their way to church on Sunday morning, quite mindful of what it took for them to press their way to "be in the service one more time."[3] They sang songs like "Lord, I Done Done What You Told Me to Do" and "I Saw the Light." Some of the songs were upbeat; others were slow and contemplative.

These people, my people, knew "what a privilege it is to carry everything to God in prayer." They knew the day-to-day struggles of poverty and racism. Having Jesus as a friend meant they could find comfort from life's trials, temptations, and troubles. They knew that though they felt "weak and heavy laden, cumbered with a load of care," they had a "Precious Savior [who was] still their refuge."[4]

Reflection: If the burdens of life seem to be weighing you down or you feel alone and discouraged, remember you have a friend in Jesus. "In his arms he'll take and shield you. You will find a solace there."[5]

Prayer: "May we ever, Lord, be bringing all to you in earnest prayer. Soon in glory bright, unclouded, there will be no need for prayer—rapture, praise, and endless worship will be our sweet portion there."[6] Amen.

Rev. Dr. Dara Cobb Lewis is former regional minister for the Christian Church (Disciples of Christ) in South Carolina and a certified pastoral counselor in Mount Holly, North Carolina.

[3] Charles Tindley, "Glad to Be in the Service," 1916.
[4] Joseph M. Scriven, "What a Friend We Have in Jesus," 1855.
[5] Ibid.
[6] Ibid.

Godspell: Prepare Ye the Way of the Lord

"The voice of one crying out in the wilderness: 'Prepare the way of the Lord; make his paths straight.'" —Matthew 3:3

There are many movies that would be great for a Lenten meditation: *Give Us Barabbas, The Robe, The Ten Commandments, The Song of Bernadette, The Passion of the Christ, Son of God*. The theatrical production I first saw as a teenager, *Godspell,* speaks loudly to me this season amidst all the separation and anxiety.

Godspell had a profound impact on how I live my life as a follower of the way of Christ. My three cousins and I were made to go to see the production at Chicago State University by my uncle and aunt, with whom I was living. Can you believe them? They made us dress up and go see a *musical* about Jesus Christ with actors dressed up like hippies and clowns, telling a story in ways I was not accustomed to!

Godspell stretched me to see Christ and his followers in new ways. Plays like *Jesus Christ, Superstar,* where we have Cynthia Erivo as Jesus Christ and Adam Lambert as Judas, continue to stretch us in good ways to ever expand the table.

Reflection: Has a limited view of Jesus Christ prevented you from being fully who God has created you to be?

Prayer: "Lord, these three things I pray: that we would see thee more clearly, love thee more dearly, and follow thee more nearly day by day."[7] Amen.

Rev. Dr. Donald K. Gillett II is general minister and president of the Christian Church (Disciples of Christ) in Kentucky.

[7] Richard of Chichester, 1253; Stephen Schwartz, "Day by Day" from *Godspell,* 1971.

The Passion: We Have Hope

Where, O death, is your victory? —1 Corinthians 15:55

The Lenten season always calls me back to the 2004 movie *The Passion of the Christ,* directed by Mel Gibson. The movie has the most in-depth and gruesome account of Jesus' journey to the cross I have ever witnessed. However, as I have grown and matured in my faith, I have come to realize that the actual sufferings of Jesus go far beyond what that movie portrayed.

The same is true of our sin. It runs deeper than we imagine. God cannot look at us because of our sin. This is detrimental to our spiritual lives. But because of the saving act of Jesus Christ on the cross, we have hope. Because of his death, burial, and resurrection, we have complete victory over sin. As we bring ourselves into this time of consciousness of our sin and Christ's sacrifice to redeem it, let us do so with humility and gratitude. God didn't leave us. God didn't throw us away. Instead, God sent us a Savior who obediently and innocently took on our sin to reconcile us back to God. So while sin runs deep, the blood of Jesus runs so much deeper.

Reflection: What are you passionate about? How does that passion reflect the undying love of God through Jesus Christ?

Prayer: Lord Jesus, thank you for your sacrifice on my behalf. May I never forget all that you paid so I could be free. May my passions reflect your grace, mercy, and love in the world. In your name we pray and give thanks. Amen.

Rev. Dikiea J. Elery is pastor at East Second Street Christian Church (Disciples of Christ) in Lexington, Kentucky.

Ben-Hur: Take the Sword Out of My Hand

Jesus said to Peter, "Put your sword back into its sheath."
—John 18:11

As part of my sabbath, I go to the movies every Friday. I'm a movie buff, and I enjoy experiencing how books and screenplays become films. One film I watch during Lent is the 1959 epic *Ben-Hur*. Admittedly, for most, this is not an Easter movie, but there is a corresponding message. Judah Ben-Hur, the main character played by Charlton Heston, is a Jewish aristocrat—in fact, a prince—during the Roman occupation. An accident results in a world-altering life for Ben-Hur. He is jailed, sold as a slave, and shipwrecked and becomes a chariot racer. We witness his anger, resentment, and lust for revenge against a Roman friend whom he feels betrayed him.

How is this about Easter? Ben-Hur's journey intersects with Jesus'. Ben-Hur receives water from Jesus, and while Jesus is carrying his cross on the path to his crucifixion, Ben-Hur tries to give Jesus some water. We witness an angry man seeking revenge becoming someone who receives healing and peace as he declares: "Almost at that moment he died, I heard him say, 'Father, forgive them, for they know not what they do.' And I felt his voice take the sword out of my hand." For many this Lenten season, we too need an encounter with our Lord to let go of anger, envy, greed, unforgiveness, resentment, and revenge. In this season, return to the cross to receive peace, love, and forgiveness.

Reflection: To whom do you need to be reconciled?

Prayer: Dear Lord, we pray for an encounter with the holy to restore our peace. Fill us with the awe, love, joy, peace, and forgiveness only made possible by the empty tomb. Amen.

Rev. Dr. Donald K. Gillett II general minister and president of the Christian Church (Disciples of Christ) in Kentucky.

Lay Not Up for Yourselves

Store up for yourselves treasures in heaven. —Matthew 6:20

When I think about the influence of the gospel according to TikTok and Instagram, I'm reminded of the paper chase that keeps many of us busy. Yes, we need money to live and care for ourselves. It's easy to see how circumstances and external influences can consume us through the pressure for financial gain. However, many examples in the Bible teach us about the consequences of the love of money. As we travel our own Lenten journey, we are encouraged to reflect on Jesus' journey to the cross. We see an example of how the desire for moneybags resulted in our Savior being sold out and Judas Iscariot making his bed in hell.

We would never consider ourselves as vain and vile as Judas. We would not dare betray our Savior for thirty silver coins, right? Or would we? Maybe it's not literally thirty silver coins that threaten to tear us away from our relationship with God, but could it be that dollar we didn't give that unhoused person we rushed past? Or that overabundance of clothing or shoes or treasures that we refuse to donate? Could it be our work schedule that won't allow time for Bible study or worship? Hear these words from the biblical text: *"Lay not up for yourselves treasures upon earth"* (Matthew 6:19 KJV).

Reflection: Where is your treasure? How is it impacting your heart for God and God's people?

Prayer: Gracious God, as we travel this Lenten journey, help us discern where we may be laying up treasures upon the earth. Give us a heart of repentance that spurs us to compassion and good stewardship. Amen.

Rev. Dikiea J. Elery is pastor at East Second Street Christian Church (Disciples of Christ) in Lexington, Kentucky.

These Praying Hands

The Lord will keep your going out and your coming in from this time on and forevermore. —Psalms 121:8

Psalm 121 is a traveler's song, a reminder that even far from home, help is near—the Lord who created heaven and earth. In the African American experience, these words hold deep, living power. From the holds of slave ships to the cotton fields, from bus boycotts to today's struggles for justice and dignity, our ancestors looked to God as their ultimate help and keeper.

We learned to look beyond the hills of hardship to see the God who stands above it all. We hold onto faith even when the road is steep and the night long. We know, as the psalmist knew, that the Lord protects us, keeps us from harm, and guards our coming and going now and forevermore.

Instead of clenched fists, we lift praying hands, remembering we are not alone. We do not succumb to hate; we surrender to a loving God who protects and leads us. Our ancestors' hands remind us that God is strong when we are weak and God will guide us when we feel lost.

Reflection: When has God replaced your clenched fists with praying hands?

Prayer: O God, our keeper and sustainer, thank you for watching over us on this long and weary journey. Remind us daily that our help comes from you, from the One who made heaven and earth. Amen.

Rev. Kevin L. McNeil is regional minister for the Christian Church (Disciples of Christ) in Tennessee.

I Lift Up My Praying Hands

I will lift up my hands to Your Word. —Psalms 119:48 (NLV)

During the forty days of Lent, I invite you to imagine praying hands. As a Black woman in medicine, my hands hold both the weight of others' pain and their quiet yet steadfast strength. With these hands, I have cheered on the hopeful to "take one more step," delivered hard truths to the fearful, and held the hands of the dying. In this Lenten season I remember that before these hands served, they *prayed.*

The image of praying hands is more than a symbol; it is my posture of surrender, my connection to God. In a world that often misjudges me by my skin, gender, and profession, I remember my worth remains anchored in God, who formed me and calls me "daughter." Recall that Jesus, too, knelt and prayed, hands clasped in obedience and agony in his final days. He knows my exhaustion, my sacrifice.

Lent is an invitation to re-center. Unclench your tired, capable hands, and lift them to the hills in care, worship, and gratitude. Before we can heal others, we must be restored. We must ask God to be a vessel of a kind of power only he can provide. Resurrection is not just on a Sunday morning. Every day we are granted breath to rise, trust, and pray to our Creator.

Reflection: In what ways will you accept the Lenten invitation to pray?

Prayer: May these praying hands remind us that God sees, hears, and redeems. Let these forty days of Lent be a return to the sacred. Amen.

Jamyl N. Walker, DNP,MSN, AGNP-C, is a nurse practitioner in geriatric and palliative care medicine at Massachusetts General Hospital in Boston, Massachusetts.

Palms to Passion: Joy and Pain

They took branches of palm trees and went out to meet him, shouting, "Hosanna! Blessed is the one who comes in the name of the Lord—the King of Israel!" —John 12:13

Palm Sunday is one of my favorite worship experiences. In churches I have attended, Palm Sunday services began with waving palm branches and singing "Hosanna!" I can recall the sense of joy we all felt as we imagined Jesus triumphantly entering Jerusalem.

But this celebration of Jesus was short-lived. Joy gave way to the tragedy of his suffering and death. While John 12:12–13 does not address this aspect of Palm Sunday, I still ponder it amid the celebrating, and I appreciate the liturgy that guides us from palms to passion.

I am United Methodist. While in seminary, I often drove a retired African American bishop and his wife to evening events because night driving was difficult for them. Once I drove them to a celebration of the bishop and his contributions to African American Methodism. During the evening, one of his closest friends did not return from the restroom. He had suffered a heart attack and fallen. The bishop was aware of this when he gave his remarks on an occasion that was supposed to be a celebration of his ministry. His words stay with me: "We must always be prepared in the midst of celebration for tragedy. It is a part of life." He shared how this is especially true for African Americans.

John 12:12–13 has new significance for me since hearing the bishop's words. We cannot separate celebration and suffering. Both are part of life, but suffering should not diminish celebration. Even as we experience suffering, we should still sing "Hosanna!" just as we do on Palm Sunday.

Reflection: What gives you hope when you experience suffering amid celebration?

Prayer: God, be with us in times of celebration and suffering. Amen.

Rev. F. Douglas Powe Jr., Ph.D, is president at Phillips Theological Seminary and Mouzon Biggs Jr. professor of Methodist studies.

Victory in the Palm

Thanks be to God, who gives us the victory through our Lord Jesus Christ. —1 Corinthians 15:57

There is a great dilemma most of us encounter at one time in our lives: when we decide to lose weight. We feel this pressure perhaps because we're not pleased with our body image, by our clothes that don't fit properly, or even from health concerns exacerbated by extra pounds. In our pursuit of change, either through diet and exercise or other prescribed treatments, what we desire most is the discipline to act in a positive way to effect the change we want.

As we work toward our worthy goals, we face not only internal forces that create impediments to our achieving victory, but also external forces that hinder us from accomplishing our objectives. Fear, anger, and despair come from our internal desire to achieve. Then we must deal with the external forces, including temptations and negative influences from others.

Palm leaves are a symbol of victory over obstacles and constraints, even those that are self-imposed. Those challenges are enemies of our souls. We face many obstacles in pursuit of faith, justice, and love and being resilient in hope. When Jesus entered Jerusalem, the palm leaves were a sign that he was the One who would overcome the oppression, injustice, and fear the people had experienced for centuries. During Lent, our journey toward victory over the enemies of our souls begins with overcoming the internal and external forces that seek to burden us. Our liberation from the bonds of captivity comes in knowing that the Jesus of then and now will give us the victory.

Reflection: What will be your pathway to victory?

Prayer: Lord, give us a resilient faith that guides us with the knowledge that you are always there to make us more than conquerors. Amen.

Rev. Dr. Edward Smith Davis, MBA, DMin., CNPM, is conference minister and chief executive for the Southern Conference, United Church of Christ.

Jesus Washed Their Feet: A Model for Service

He poured water into a basin and began to wash the disciples' feet. —John 13:5

In first-century Palestine, the daily journey through town and from city to city was often taken on foot. Feet got dirty. The soles of one's feet would be hardened by exposure to dust and stones. One of the most important acts of hospitality was washing guests' feet as they entered one's home. This was both a gift and a necessity. Touching another's feet was also an act of intimacy. Today we might cringe at the idea of washing someone's feet. We don't really want to see—let alone touch—another's feet. We joke about people's feet being dirty and smelly, their toes "all jacked up."

On the night he was betrayed, Jesus girded himself with a towel and knelt before his disciples to perform this most intimate act of service. Peter was outdone at the thought that Jesus would stoop to wash his feet, but Jesus was showing that leaders must first be servants of all. Perhaps Jesus hoped Peter would take a towel and wash the other disciples' feet, not simply indulge in receiving the service Jesus provided. Peter had not yet learned the lesson: it is in the serving, not the receiving, that we are shaped as leaders.

Jesus' model for humility and service is more important today than ever. Service often involves engaging in intimate ways we would prefer not to. At the heart of foot-washing is the humility that signals to another: "I love you as Jesus loves all of us. I am willing to kneel, to wash, to dry, to serve, just as Jesus did." Service involves submission to the humanity of others, embracing their "jacked up" bits and pieces, and acknowledging that we all have dirty feet and we're all in need of care.

Reflection: How have you modeled service in your ministry?

Prayer: Dear God, as we serve one another, let us be mindful of Jesus' teaching and yield ourselves to acts of humble service for our community. Amen.

Rev. Teresa Hord Owens is general minister and president of the Christian Church (Disciples of Christ) in the United States and Canada.

In the Season of Unleavened Bread

Seven days you shall eat unleavened bread. —Exodus 13:6

We gather at the table of memory, where the bread is flat but the story is full. The Israelites fled Egypt with unleavened bread because there wasn't time to wait for it to rise. Women have always known how to wait. We wait with hands in dough, with hearts stretched across generations, with prayers whispered between the cracks of silence.

They didn't name us in the upper room. But we were there: kneading, baking, preparing. The unleavened bread didn't rise, but we did. We rise like Maya said: in defiance, in dignity, in divine rhythm. This bread, stripped of yeast, reminds us of urgency, of escape, of the holy hush before liberation. But it also reminds us of the sacred pause, the waiting that teaches, the stillness that births revelation.

In this season, we rise in the midst of grief, joy, injustice, and healing. We rise not because the world gives us permission, but because Christ dwells in our rising. He is in the waiting, in the wellness we reclaim, in the redemptive self-love we stir into our souls like warm water into flour.

We rise with a communal ethic, not just for ourselves, but for the ones who come after, for the ones still kneading in the back, still unnamed, still holy.

Let the bread stay flat. Let it speak of haste and hope.

Reflection: What can you do usher in the holy?

Prayer: Dear God, may the bread remind us: we are the leaven. We are the rising. We are the ones who wait, and still—we rise. Amen.

Rev. Virzola Law is pastor at Northway Christian Church (Disciples of Christ) and chair of the board for Brite Divinity School in Dallas, Texas.

Unleavened Bread: A Symbol of Remembrance, Resistance, and Renewal

Let us celebrate the festival, not with the old yeast ...
but with the unleavened bread of sincerity and truth.
—1 Corinthians 5:8

During the forty days (excluding Sundays) leading up to the day Christians celebrate Jesus' resurrection, many engage in spiritual and ecclesial practices that acknowledge the destructive effects of brokenness, sin, and systemic injustices on their lives and communities. Spiritual disciplines such as fasting, prayer, introspection, self-denial, and sacrifice serve as reminders that missing the mark remains a fundamental part of the human experience. Lent invites people to turn toward God by recalibrating their hearts and ethics so God's faithfulness, liberation, and renewal can guide their journey.

The Exodus stories about Passover and the Feast of Unleavened Bread emphasize God's faithfulness and humanity's sacred response. Remembering and embracing these acts of liberation encourages resistance to a corrupt culture and oppressive practices. Israel's instructions to avoid eating leavened bread taught them and future generations to reject sin, pride, and ethical commitments that hinder human and communal flourishing. Eating unleavened bread symbolized loyalty to a mighty God. When people resist sin and evil in their lives and communities today, opportunities to thrive and find wholeness become possible. As 1 Corinthians 5:8 explicitly suggests, eating unleavened bread is more than a ritual to observe; it is a way of living and existing in the world.

Reflection: As you journey through the Lenten season, what leavened bread-like realities are you willing to resist, let go of, or transform?

Prayer: Dear God, thank you for making liberation possible for me and my community. Help me live as "unleavened bread," a symbol of faith in my current context. Amen.

Rev. Derrick L. Perkins Sr. is director of congregational vitality and innovation for Disciples Home Missions.

Not My Will But Thine

"My Father, if it is possible, let this cup pass from me; yet not what I want but what you want." —Matthew 26:39

I'm sure we've all seen the painting of Jesus praying in the Garden of Gethsemane on the night of his betrayal and arrest. With his folded hands resting atop a rock, he raises his eyes beseechingly heavenward. He knows what lies ahead of him. And he dreads it, all of it—his seizure, his "trial," the beatings he would undergo, the crown of thorns they would jam on his head, and finally his crucifixion. In this moment where he encountered a very human dread of pain and suffering, He turned to God with a prayer that "this cup" would pass from him. He himself is our rock, the One on whom we lean and depend in times of trial and trouble, and yet he needed support, too. So he turned to God, asking if there could possibly be another solution, another way to save and redeem God's people. He was getting desperate, but still he prayed the most effective prayer anyone can utter: "Not my will, oh Lord, but thine." Then he heard the clash of swords and the tramping of footsteps, and he knew the time had come. He rose from his knees and, fortified by his time with God, turned around to meet his fate.

Reflection: Do you find it difficult to echo Jesus' prayer, "Not my will but thine"? During Lent, practice saying it and feel the hand of God upon you, steadying you like a rock.

Prayer: Dear God, my prayer is Jesus'. In every facet of my life, may it be your will, not mine, that is done, and may I rest and rely upon the rock, our Lord and Savior, Jesus Christ. Amen.

Rev. Tanya J. Tyler is pastor at First Christian Church (Disciples of Christ) in Ruidoso, New Mexico.

Lifting Up the Cross

He himself bore our sins in his body on the cross.
—1 Peter 2:24

The cross has great significance for me. When I think of it, these words come to mind: sacrifice, atonement, forgiveness, and reconciliation.

Sacrifice. Jesus died on the cross for you and me. God loved us so much that God reconciled with humanity by offering his only begotten Son to die for our sins.

Atonement. This is the process of making amends and restoring a broken relationship. It involves the removal of sin and its consequences, allowing for fellowship with God.

Forgiveness. The cross is central to the Christian understanding of forgiveness, signifying God's forgiveness of humanity's sins. While Jesus was on the cross, he prayed for forgiveness for those crucifying him. This reminds us to forgive those who may wrong us.

Reconciliation. Reconciliation involves seeking and extending forgiveness and actively working toward restoring broken relationships.

The cross is a powerful Lenten symbol. I am humbled, thankful, and grateful when I see a cross. I embrace these sentiments when I wear mine. Humbled because as Jesus was ridiculed, betrayed, humiliated, and abused, he remained meek and continued his mission. Thankful that God gave humankind a chance for restoration through Jesus' sacrifice. Grateful that when we accept Jesus as our Savior, we are given a new life and the Holy Spirit as our Comforter.

Reflection: Why do you wear a cross? What sentiments does wearing a cross evoke for you?

Prayer: Dear God, my prayer is a familiar song: "At the cross, at the cross where I first saw the light, and the burden of my heart rolled away, it was there by faith I received my sight, and now I am [thankful, humbled, and grateful] all the day!"[8] Amen.

Dr. Sheila R. Morris is a retired Chicago Public Schools principal and lives in Clarksville, Tennessee.

[8] Isaac Watts, "At the Cross," 1707.

Suffer Much

He has borne our griefs and carried our sorrows.
—Isaiah 53:4 (NKJV)

The root word for suffering means to bear with, undergo, or endure. It means we will go through some things in our lives. Suffering suggests we have experienced something that is not only unpleasant, but traumatic, tragic, and potentially life-changing.

When I was a congregational pastor, I'd ask church members to suggest topics about which they wanted to hear a sermon during the summer months. Every time, without fail, several members would request a sermon on suffering, usually along the lines of why horrible things happen to good people. An assumption in the request was a desire to understand the purpose of suffering. Is it punishment for disappointing God? Is it a consequence for behaving so unrighteously that the righteous One demanded vengeance?

No, suffering is not punishment. Suffering is part of the human condition. We cannot move from birth to death without enduring physical, spiritual, mental, or emotional pain.

As human beings, we will find ourselves in difficult and unbearable situations. But we do not suffer alone. The One whom we believe has borne our griefs and carried our sorrows is with us and will not leave us. If we can stand it, suffering leads to hope and new life. "Suffering produces endurance, and endurance produces character, and character produces hope, and hope does not disappoint us" (Romans 5:3–5).

Reflection: Rev. Dr. Martin Luther King Jr. said undeserved suffering is redemptive. When has suffering led to gratitude, personal growth, or positive change for you?

Prayer: God who bears us up when life is falling around us, continue to be present with us and endure with us until peace and healing come, then stay with us still. Amen.

Rev. Dr. LaTaunya M. Bynum is regional minister of the Christian Church (Disciples of Christ) in Northern California-Nevada.

Witness of the Lily

The flowers appear on the earth. —Song of Solomon 2:12

When was the last time you looked at a lily? When was the last time you admired its stature, inhaled its fragrance, appreciated its beauty? Was it the last time you went to church on Resurrection Sunday?

I don't know a lot about flowers. I just know the names of the ones that brighten my day and put a smile on my face. Flowers enhance the decor of rooms, liven up gardens, and make great gifts. The person who receives flowers feels special. What might someone intend to say when they choose to send or display lilies?

Lilies represent purity, hope, comfort, renewal, and new beginnings. Thus, it is no surprise that lilies are shared during times of grief and on the Sunday we celebrate the resurrection of our Lord. The lily's drooping nature reminds us there is still beauty amid the tearful moments. It reminds us that just as our Creator cares for the lilies of the fields, we can trust we will be cared for during our pain. The lily's shape has been likened to a trumpet. That might remind us about the sound we will hear when we are caught up to meet the Lord.

As we reflect on all the symbols of this Lenten season, I pray that we are especially encouraged by the presence of lilies throughout our sanctuaries. They gracefully hold the tension of the crucifixion, death, and resurrection of our Lord.

Reflection: To whom will you send a lily this season?

Prayer: Dear awesome God, may we continue to see your favor in the lilies and other flowers that make us smile. May we seek joy in the beauty of those symbols that remind us of a resurrected Christ. Amen.

Rev. Dr. Delesslyn A. Kennebrew, J.D., MDiv., is administrative secretary of the National Convocation and associate general minister and president of the Christian Church (Disciples of Christ).

Consider the Lilies of the Fields

... how they grow. —Matthew 6:28

Lilies of the Fields is a 1963 movie starring Sidney Poitier. The movie is considered groundbreaking because it starred a Black man in a leading role. Poitier played the role of a handyman with such dignity, skill, and agency that he received the Oscar for Best Actor that year.

As a young person watching the movie, I did not understand the significance of Poitier's powerful performance, the racial undertones of the movie, or the radical behavior of the Catholic nuns in it. Both the handyman and the nuns were claiming freedom from tradition in the context of a Hollywood movie. What I noticed then and recall now is the movie's title. I wanted to know where I could find lilies in a field. Did they look like the ones in the movie? Did they grow like the plants my aunt and grandparents were always watering and separating and putting in jars to grow new plants?

Growing in my faith, I came to appreciate descriptions of God as "the rose of Sharon," "the lily of the field," or, as scripture says, "wildflowers" spreading in the field. Both the strength and beauty of the lily are present. Like the poinsettia during Advent and Christmas, the lily is a powerful Lenten and Easter symbol. The lily's delicate strength reminds us that God will provide, protect, and offer comfort in times of joy and tumult.

Reflection: Have you noticed the Easter lily's strength and beauty? How does it mirror the freedom of the Gospel?

Prayer: Dear God, you have offered us beauty and strength in the Easter lily. May we know that beauty and strength as we live and mature through life's struggles. Amen.

Rev. Dr. Charisse L. Gillett is president at Lexington Theological Seminary.

Persevering Faith in Times of Trouble

My help comes from the Lord, who made heaven and earth.
—Psalms 121:2

Lent affords us the opportunity to remember and find inspiration in the spiritual resilience Jesus modeled in the salvific act of redeeming humanity. Let us remember the sacrifice of so many in the African American past who, inspired by Christ's witness, activated a faith response in their pursuit of equality.

The image of Jesus on the cross reminds us that the King of kings and Lord of lords was mocked and endured the agony of physical pain. For many on the African American Christian faith journey, remembering Jesus' journey gives us courage in our personal and community trouble.

What can we do to persevere spiritually in times of trouble? This is the same question asked in Psalm 121. In times of trouble, where does our help come from? The psalmist reminds us our help "comes from the Lord, who made heaven and earth" (121:2). Trusting God in times of trouble requires that we have an assuring faith. We must have courage and remain encouraged enough to look up spiritually and metaphorically to the source of our help and the source of our faith—God alone.

Reflection: How can the African American faith journey serve as a persevering blueprint for navigating trouble?

Prayer: As we navigate seasons of wilderness wanderings and crossroads of faith and unbelief, let us remember the God of our persevering faith as the source of our help in times of trouble. The same God who created us is the same God who is keeping us. Amen.

Rev. Dr. Perzavia T. Praylow is assistant professor of historical theology and director of Black Church Studies and the Black Church Cornerstone Collaborative at Louisville Presbyterian Theological Seminary.

Following at a Distance

Peter was following him at a distance. —Matthew 26:58

These are confusing times for people trying to figure out exactly what qualifies as Christian. There are those who claim the mantle of leadership in church and society, cloaking themselves in religious verbiage and righteously opposing everything Jesus stood for in word and deed. We have seen them do this in our homes, in church, in our communities, and in government. In an upside-down world, it is not what we say but what we do that is the testimony of our faith.

In this Lenten season, we must ask: How closely are we following Jesus? Are we following at a "safe" distance, or are we close enough for Jesus' blood to splatter on us? Jesus told us the greatest commandment is to love God and the second greatest is to love our neighbor.

"Neighbor" is not geographical but relational. Our neighbors extend to other humans, animals, and plant life. We were created by God, we belong to God, so we should glorify God.

Following Jesus is sweat-on-your-brow, dirt-under-your-fingernails kind of work. I cannot pull people out of the mud of life if I am not willing to get a little muddy myself. God did not call us to be spectators but participants in the valleys and deserts as well as the hilltop moments in our neighbors' lives.

Reflection: How might you be a neighbor for those suffering in your midst?

Prayer: Dear God, we pray for those in places of power that they might not use your words to betray your people. We pray to be able to discern in an upside-down world what is right, what is true, and what is good. Amen.

Rev. Dr. Jesse Jackson Jr. is pastor at East Sixth Street Christian Church (Disciples of Christ) in Oklahoma City, Oklahoma.

Expect God's Provision

"Cast the net to the right side of the boat, and you will find some [fish]." —John 21:6

The fish as a Christian symbol is an image that captures the psalmist's affirmation that God responds in real and relevant ways to our circumstances. Three stories in the New Testament use the symbol of fish to remind us of God's provision. In the story of "The Coin in the Fish," Jesus sends the disciples to catch a fish and retrieve a coin from its mouth to pay taxes. In the story "Loaves and Fish Feed the Multitude," the disciples are sent to gather available resources and share what they find among the people indiscriminately. In the story of "Fish for Breakfast," Jesus tells the disciples to switch sides of the boat they are fishing from, risking the condition of the nets, to gather the large catch.

In each pericope, the disciples face the challenges of using available resources for concerns of daily life. In every case, they are encouraged to expect God's provision. They must move from contemplation to action, consider the needs of many, and change their usual practices. The stories of fish remind us that changing our perspective to one of expecting God's provision is a realistic and relevant response to the particulars of our circumstance.

Reflection: When does our commitment to tradition fade into routine and prevent us from realizing God's provision?

Prayer: Loving God, help me expect your presence and provision and to choose to act in ways that bear witness to your love and faithfulness. Amen.

Rev. Vinnetta Golphin-Wilkerson is Commission on Ministry chair for the Central Rocky Mountain Region of the Christian Church (Disciples of Christ).

African American Heritage Hymnal Litany 67: Holy Week

Lord, we celebrate this Holy Week by tracing Your steps from Palm Sunday to Easter Sunday. Amid the waving of palms, You rode into Jerusalem. Your triumphant entry marked the beginning of our redemption.

O blessed Savior, we thank You for our redemption.

Lord, on that Monday, You rebuked and confronted unrighteousness by cleansing the temple.

O, Holy and Righteous One, we thank You for our redemption.

Lord, on Tuesday and Wednesday, You proclaimed that when You are lifted up from the earth, You will draw all people to You.

Lord Jesus, we thank You for our redemption.

Jesus, on Thursday, You celebrated the Passover and instituted the Lord's Supper. You washed the disciples' feet, promised the Holy Spirit, and healed the ear of Malchus.

O Great Healer, we thank You for our redemption.

Lord, on that same night, Judas betrayed You for thirty pieces of silver. You were arrested and brought before Caiaphas, but showed no anger against these men.

Forgiving God, we thank You for our redemption.

Lord, on Friday, Peter denied You three times. Pilate did not want any part of Your crucifixion. You were mocked and spat upon and Judas hanged himself because of his betrayal. Lord, You accepted the thief on the cross, and died at Calvary because of Your love for us.

"Were you there when they crucified my Lord? Sometimes it causes me to tremble, tremble, tremble."

Lord, when You died on on Calvary, darkness covered the whole land, the earth shook, the veil of the temple split in two, the thunder rumbled, and the graves opened. The centurion said, "Certainly this man was innocent."

"Were you there when they pierced Him in His side? Sometimes it causes me to tremble, tremble, tremble."

Lord, come Sunday, people all over the world will join together to celebrate the power of Your resurrection. We know the pain and suffering of Good Friday, and we thank You for helping us experience the joy of Easter. Because You live, we can face tomorrow.

Lord Jesus, we thank You for paying the cost of righteousness.

Delores Carpenter is general editor of the African American Heritage Hymnal.

A Crown of Thorns

After twisting some thorns into a crown, they put it on his head. —Matthew 27:29

I saw a flower called the crown of thorns many years ago in Africa. It's a breathtakingly beautiful flower. The plant features colorful bracts of red, pink, yellow, orange, and white. It thrives in sunny conditions and blooms throughout the year.

The crown of thorns that was fashioned for Jesus on Good Friday stands in stark contrast to the crown of thorns flower. It did not burst with color or majesty. Jesus' crown was a drab brown with thorns that drew blood at the slightest touch. No beauty to behold here. This crown mirrored the ugliness of that dark day when our Savior died.

The soldiers intended to mock Jesus. The prickly crown of thorns pushed down over his brow was meant to bring pain and suffering. It was designed to embarrass, degrade, and shame him. Little did the soldiers know that what they meant for evil God would use for our good. (Recall Joseph's words to his brothers in Genesis 50:20.) The fact that I am writing over two thousand years later about that crown is sufficient evidence of how God has transformed ugly into beautiful.

Jesus' crown of thorns now looks more like that flower called the crown of thorns. This new life we live in Jesus is breathtaking. It calls for singing anew the lines of the hymn "Lead Me to Calvary"[9]:

King of my life I crown thee now; thine shall the glory be.

Lest I forget thy thorn-crowned brow, lead me to Calvary.

Reflection: What seemingly evil thing can you see being used for good?

Prayer: God, open my eyes to see your majesty and glory. May I never forget the love that was poured out for me on Calvary. Amen.

Rev. Dr. William L. Lee is chair of the Board of Trustees for Lexington Theological Seminary.

[9] Jennie E. Hussey, "Lead Me to Calvary," 1921.

Take Up His Cross

"If any want to become my followers, let them deny themselves and take up their cross and follow me."
—Matthew 16:24

The Lenten season is a time of reflection and meditation. It is a call to action to create change in our lives. Many churches are filled with Lenten rituals, such as changing the liturgical colors on the altar, helping those in need, fasting, and spending time in prayer to connect with God. I had never heard of nor practiced Lent until I became an adult. When I was young, the Easter season was filled with the anticipation of egg hunts, ruffled socks, pretty dresses, and seeing what the bunny would bring. While the traditions were different, one thing remains true for both: the anticipation of something exciting that marks a transition from one season to the next.

When we reflect on the sacrifice Jesus made on the cross, it does not bring the same smiles, joy, and excitement as the Lenten/Easter season we are familiar with. It reminds us of the shame and heartache and becomes a call for repentance when we realize it was our sin that led Jesus to die on our behalf.

When Jesus told his disciples to take up their crosses and follow him, it meant that just as Jesus had to give up his life as a sacrifice, we are required to give up anything that hinders us from fully serving God. To follow someone means you trust the guide and the direction in which that person is going. Life can be tough, but if we trust our guide and sacrifice our own agenda, we can be excited about the transition from pain to purpose.

Reflection: What memories do you have of the Lenten and Easter seasons?

Prayer: Lord, thank you for your Son, Jesus, who paid the ultimate sacrifice on the cross. Help us honor you not only with our words but also in how we live. Amen.

Rev. Kimberley Proctor-White is a certified clinical mental health professional in Nashville, Tennessee.

Seven Last Words

He said, "It is finished." —John 19:30

Attending a "Seven Last Words of Christ" service on Good Friday is part of my Lenten tradition. Hearing the different voices interpreting these sayings gives fresh meaning to the scriptures: *Woman, behold thy son—son, behold thy mother. Father, into thy hands I commend my spirit. My God, my God, why hast thou forsaken me? Today you will be with me in paradise. I thirst. Father, forgive them. It is finished.*

As I have grown older, my attention has shifted from the way "personal privilege" taken by those invited to speak lengthens the service to thinking deeply about the range of emotions Jesus felt.

Facing imminent death, Jesus expressed bewilderment, assured others they would have everlasting life, and asked God to forgive those who were simply wrong. In death, Jesus continued to give. Recent experience helped me realize anew how difficult it is to lose loved ones to earthly death. Imagine those loved ones saying out loud, "God, why have you forsaken me to this cruel disease?" Imagine a loved one saying to you on their deathbed, "Forgive them. Give them another chance." Imagine nearing acceptance that your time on earth is ending and saying to your family, "It is finished. I must go." Imagine recalling the words "Son, behold your mother; mother, behold your son" and in your last moments whispering the same to your family, admonishing them to hold each other.

Earthly death is final, but the resurrection of the spirit is possible for those who understand that only a sovereign God can say when it is finished.

Reflection: Which of the seven last sayings of Christ speaks most deeply to you?

Prayer*:* Dear God, give us the maturity and faith to live in our Good Friday moments, knowing that new life awaits.

Rev. Dr. Charisse L. Gillett is president at Lexington Theological Seminary.

Maundy Thursday: Our Mandate for This Day

I give you a new commandment, that you love one another. Just as I have loved you, you also should love one another.
—John 13:34

The ancient designation of this day, this night, is "Maundy," a form of the word "mandate." What is a mandate? It is a command, a demand, an order, something required. It is mandatory rather than optional. No choice.

What is our mandate on this day? To love one another even as Christ has loved us.

In John's gospel, we get a different take on things than the three synoptic writers offer. John tells of a meal, too, prefaced with a foot-washing, but his focus is more on the show and tell: "This is what it looks like when you love one another."

"Love one another" is our mandate for this day. As we break the body of Jesus once again in the act of taking the bread, may we remember his command to love one another. Let us remember the example he has given us in the gospel of John of how to take care of one another. Love shown in service rather than being served tells the world who the true disciples of Jesus are. Let us do so in remembrance of our Lord.

Reflection: How do you show love as a disciple of Jesus?

Prayer: Thank you, God, for Jesus' new commandment. Help us to love you and others daily so that we can show the world true Christian discipleship.

Rev. Dr. Amariah McIntosh is pastor at
Phillips Chapel CME Church in Akron, Ohio.

Forgiving and Moving Forward

Just as the Lord has forgiven you, so you also must forgive.
—Colossians 3:13

Beloved, forgiveness is not forgetting. It is not weakness. It is holy resistance. Forgiveness is resisting the temptation to hold on to anger, wrath, and bitterness. It is being released from the desire to take matters into your own hands. Forgiveness is responding in love. It is respecting kingdom principles. Forgiveness reflects God's nature. We promote healing and unity and embrace a new lifestyle.

For African Americans, forgiveness is enjoined with a deep history of injustice—enslavement, segregation, generational trauma, personal wounds carried silently. Yet, as we journey through Lent, we are reminded that forgiveness is not a surrender to pain—it is a path to freedom.

Jesus, nailed to the cross by state violence, cried out, "Father, forgive them." That divine cry echoes through our history—from the songs sung in the cotton fields to the marches in Selma, from kitchen-table prayers to sanctuary pulpits. Forgiveness is not about excusing wrongs; it is about refusing to let hatred define us.

To forgive is to trust God's justice more than our own vengeance. It is to unclench the fists of our souls so we can hold on to joy, peace, and hope. Forgiveness doesn't erase the memory—it heals it. It says: *I remember what you did, and I choose not to let it control me anymore.* In forgiving, we become like Christ: wounded but still loving. Through his love, we reclaim our power and our purpose.

Reflection: This Lent, ask yourself: What anger have I been nurturing? Who have I refused to release?

Prayer: God of our weary years and silent tears, heal our memories, restore our joy, and help us forgive as you forgave us. Amen.

Rev. Dr. Maxine L. Thomas is co-pastor at Saint Andrew AME Church in Memphis, Tennessee, and founder and executive director of Sisters Keeping the Covenant.

The Scars Tell a Story

"Put your finger here and see my hands. Reach out your hand and put it in my side." —John 20:27

Rebecca, my granddaughter, noticed a scar on my leg. "Papa, how did you get that scar?" she asked. I explained that when I was a boy, I fell on a sharp object and cut my leg. "Do you remember when it happened? Does it hurt?" she queried. Yes, I remember when it happened, and no, it does not hurt now. The cut is healed, but it left this scar.

On Resurrection Day, Thomas wasn't present when Jesus revealed himself to his comrades. When they told Thomas they had seen Jesus, he declared, "Unless I see the marks of the nails in his hands, and put my finger in the marks of the nails and my hand in his side, I will not believe" (John 20:25).

Two weeks later, Jesus appeared again. Jesus said to Thomas, "Put your finger here and see my hands. Reach out your hand and put it in my side. Do not doubt but believe." Thomas responded, "My Lord and my God!" (John 20:27–28).

On the day of his resurrection, the nails that were used to crucify Jesus were gone, but the scars remained. Thus, on that first Easter, there was no argument that the crucified Christ was very much alive. Just as my scar reminds me of an event in my life, Jesus' scars were irrefutable evidence that the person standing before them was indeed the risen Lord.

Reflection: What scars do you carry on your body and in your soul? Have you asked Jesus to heal them?

Prayer: Dear God, our scars testify to resurrection. Remind us to wear them as badges of honor, indicating we have been healed through Christ. Amen.

Rev. Dr. William L. Lee is chair of the Board of Trustees for Lexington Theological Seminary.

The Tomb is Empty

He is not here. —Matthew 28:6

The empty tomb stands as a powerful declaration of God's promise fulfilled. The stone placed at the entrance was meant to seal Jesus in—to silence the truth and stop the prophecy from being realized. Yet, in God's divine plan, the stone was not a barrier but a symbol. Its removal represents the lifting of everything that separates us from God.

When the women went to the tomb, they expected to find death. Instead, they were met with life—the angel's proclamation: *"He has risen"* (Matthew 28:6 NIV). These words became a turning point in history. They announced not only Jesus' victory over the grave but also our hope for redemption and renewal.

The empty tomb proclaims death is not the end. In our own lives, we face moments of deep pain, fear, brokenness, or uncertainty. Yet, just as the stone was rolled away, God continues to remove the barriers that keep us bound. He brings life out of death, joy out of sorrow, and hope out of despair. The resurrection affirms that our faith is not in vain—it is anchored in the transforming power of God. In African American pulpits across the world, the proclamation "Early one Sunday morning, he got up with all power in his hands" reminds us of the victory we have in Jesus Christ. Let us rejoice in the truth of the resurrection. The tomb is empty—and because of that, our hearts are full.

Reflection: When has your tomb been empty? What did you do to replenish your spirit?

Prayer: Dear God, remind us that in all circumstances, the tomb is empty and we have access to a power that defies death. Amen.

Rev. LaVeeshia S. Pryor is pastor at St. Paul African Methodist Episcopal Church in Frankfort, Kentucky.

Belonging

They saw a charcoal fire there, with fish on it, and bread.
—John 21:9

Fish and the Christian faith are deeply rooted in scripture and tradition. "The sign of the fish" conveys belonging. Christians used the symbol "*ichthys*" (Greek for fish) as an acronym for "*Iesous Christos Theou Yios Soter*" (Jesus Christ, Son of God, Savior) to identify Jesus' followers.

Lent is a time to prepare for the resurrection through repentance, self-examination, and growth in spiritual disciplines. I cherish the annual fish fry held every Monday after Easter—gatherings that foster deeper relationships with the risen Christ and the community, featuring fish, bread, and collards. These meals and the genuine fellowship celebrate belonging to a greater purpose.

John 21:9 describes Jesus' third post-resurrection appearance. Betrayed by Judas, denied by Peter, abandoned by his disciples, Jesus chose forgiveness instead of judgment. Rather than allowing their isolation, Jesus insisted on their belonging to the beloved community. Standing on the shore, Jesus called them to cast their nets on the right side of the boat, transforming their catch. He invited them to the fireside, where he had cooked fish and bread, redefining their vocations.

Reflection: Read John 21 in its entirety. Is Lent meant to call for intentional introspection, challenging us to redefine our will in service to authentic discipleship?

Prayer: Merciful and forgiving God, guide our reflections on our true purpose as we navigate life's waters. May this season of Lent and resurrection inspire us to seek your will and redefine our hearts in service to you. Amen.

Rev. Dr. Marcus L. Leathers is regional minister of the Christian Church (Disciples of Christ) in the Capital Area.